Jay Jay

Xulon Press
2301 Lucien Way #415
Maitland, FL 32751
407.339.4217
www.xulonpress.com

© 2019 by Cristy L. Baird

All rights reserved solely by the author. The author guarantees all contents are original and do not infringe upon the legal rights of any other person or work. No part of this book may be reproduced in any form without the permission of the author. The views expressed in this book are not necessarily those of the publisher.

Unless otherwise indicated, Scripture quotations taken from the Holy Bible, New Living Translation (NLT). Copyright ©1996, 2004, 2007 by Tyndale House Foundation. Used by permission of Tyndale House Publishers, Inc.

Printed in the United States of America.

ISBN-13: 978-1-54566-345-5

*C*risty was a girl who had a great love for animals. She enjoyed their friendships, and always had the best laughs with her animal friends.

Cristy's special friend was a little dog named Zachery.

Zachery and Cristy went everywhere together; they even went to work together.

Cristy L. Baird

    Zachery did not have a mommy or daddy. When Zachery was a little puppy, Cristy helped him to walk, eat, and play. Cristy was there for Zachery whenever he needed her.

JAY JAY

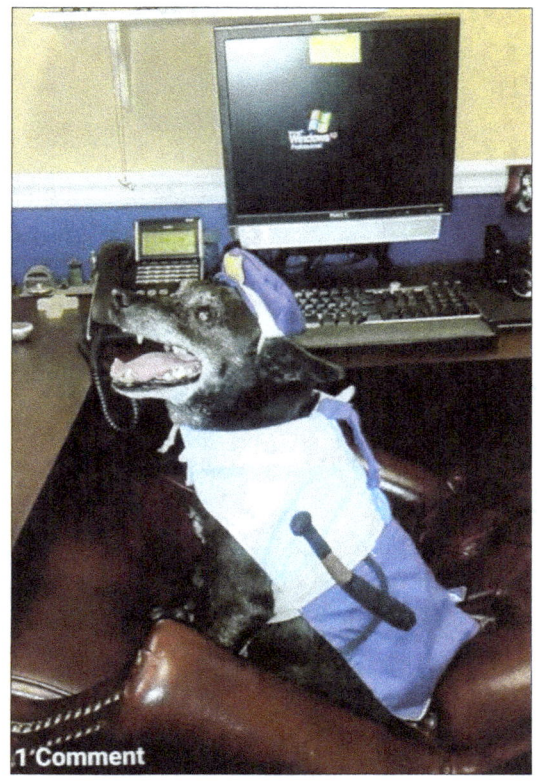

The two friends had many adventures together. Zachery loved to chase the birds, but he was afraid of thunderstorms. When the thunderstorms came, Zachery would shake, shake, shake. Cristy would find him and hold him tight when the thunder sounded.

Everything was always better when the two of them were together.

Many, many years passed. Cristy and Zachery were getting older. Cristy's bones were aching, and some of Zachery's bones were aching, too.

One day during "snuggle time" Zachery looked up at Cristy and said, "I am really tired. I think I am going to take a nap."

Cristy replied, "I love you SO much Bubba!"

Zachery closed his little eyes, took a breath, and let it go. That was it – Zachery's last moment in this world.

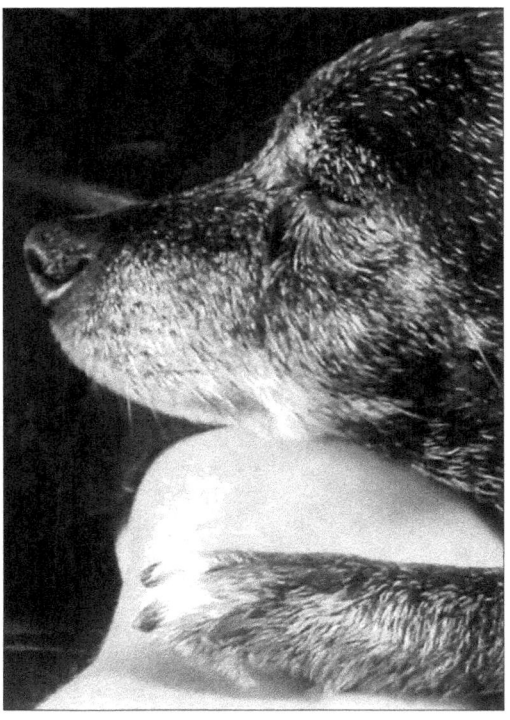

Cristy was so sad. What was she going to do without her little buddy? She said to herself, "What am I going to do without my little buddy? Who am I going to play with? Why couldn't Zachery stay with me anymore? Cristy did not understand why

God would let her love the little dog so much. Why did she have to lose him, when she needed him so much? Why did her little "snuggle buddy" have to go?

Everyday Cristy cried and cried. She missed holding Zachery in her arms. She missed stealing sweet kisses from him. Her eyes hurt from crying so much.

One night as Cristy knelt by the side of her bed, she started talking to God. "Please God, can you help me? I am so sad and lonely. I do not understand why I am hurting so badly. Zachery and I loved and cared for each other. Now, he is gone. What is the reason for this? I need to know why. Will I ever see him again? Please, Lord, help my heart heal. Please help my mind have some peace. I miss Zachery so much! I do thank you for all the many blessings you have given to me, but most of all, thank you for sending Zachery to me. I know he now has wings and can fly with the birds. Tell Zachery to fly high. Fly high my little angel dog. Fly high in the sky"

That night as Cristy slept, she started to dream. In her dream she was in a beautiful meadow surrounded by daisies. Suddenly, the daisies began to move. Something was running toward her! Whatever it was, it was getting closer and closer! A beam of sun shined down and opened a pathway in the flowers. There was Zachery running as fast as he could toward her. Zachery's tongue was hanging out of his mouth, and his tail was wagging.

With a big smile on her face Cristy dropped to her knees and held out her arms. Zachery leaped into Cristy's arms and began licking her face. She was laughing so hard that she fell back into the daisies. Words could not describe the joy the two friends were feeling. This joyful reunion of the two best friends was wonderful. While laughing and laughing the two began to play, running through the fields chasing each other.

Suddenly Cristy woke up. She looked everywhere in her bedroom, and called for Zachery, too. Zachery was not there! She knew at that moment all the time spent playing in the flowers with Zachery was just a dream.

Cristy spoke to God again. "Why, God? Why would you let me get hurt again? You know how much I miss Zachery."

Cristy was surprised by a roar of thunder. She could see a big storm was coming, when she looked out her window. The lightening strike was extremely loud. The wind blew so hard the trees bent over and the leaves flew everywhere, while heavy rain pelted down. Cristy thought how frightened Zachery would have been with the storm crashing about. But,

Zachery was not here. He no longer needed her to protect him and keep him safe from the storm. Cristy felt such sadness as the storm rumbled on.

Finally, the storm began to move on and the rain lessened. Cristy could see a break in the clouds. A small ray of sunlight was shining through the break. Suddenly, Cristy heard a noise, but did not know what it was. As the sky continued to clear she heard the noise again. She went to the door, opened it slowly, looked outside, but did not see anything. When she looked down she saw a very tiny baby bird.

The tiny Blue Jay was all alone.

Cristy looked around for its mother and daddy, but they were nowhere to be found. Cristy bent down and scooped up the precious little bird. The very small little bird was shaking.

"There, there little one, the storm is gone now. I will protect you," said Cristy. She placed the little bird on her chest. In no time the little Blue Jay snuggled next to her and fell fast asleep.

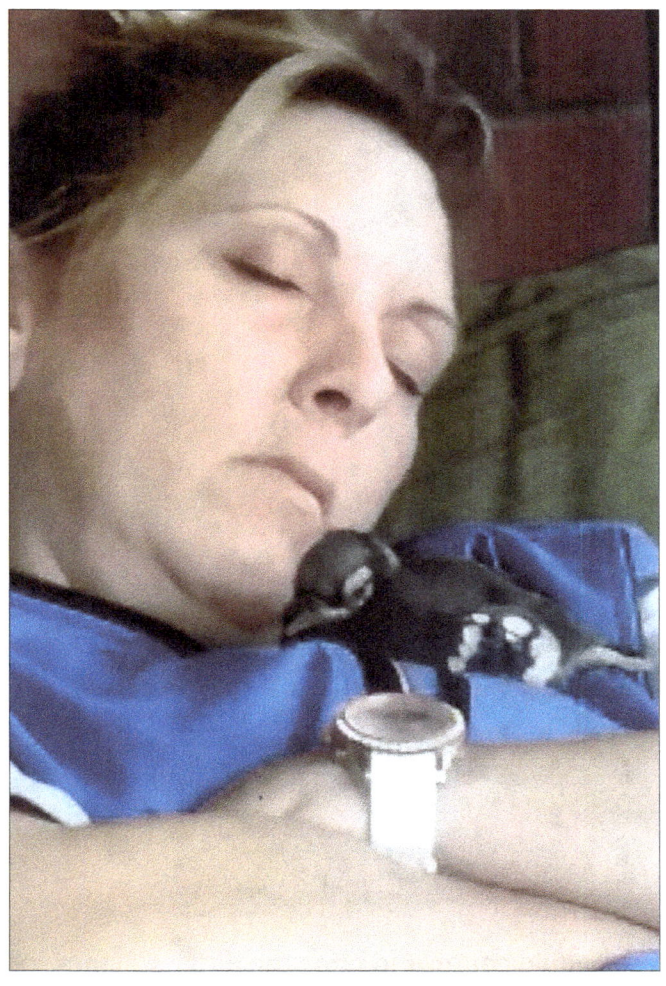

Cristy smiled for the first time in a very long while.

Before long the tiny bird awakened and began to chirp. "Chirp, chirp, chirp! Chirp, chirp, chirp! I'm hungry," she chirped.

Cristy got up, went outside, and began looking for worms to feed the tiny bird. Every twenty minutes the little bird went "chirp, chirp, chirp" to tell Cristy she was hungry again.

Cristy would get up and bring the bird bugs and worms to eat. There was no time to rest. She decided to name the little bird Jay Jay, because the little bird was a Blue Jay. Happiness shined in the little bird's eyes, and it fluttered its wings.

Each day brought changes. Jay Jay was getting stronger and stronger. Soon Jay Jay was able to hold onto tree branches, and she was getting very good at balancing. Cristy showed Jay Jay how to catch her own bugs. At night Jay Jay would sleep in a special bed made from grasses and twigs. Cristy even noticed how well Jay Jay was flapping her wings. One day Cristy told Jay Jay, "I think it is time for you to try to fly today."

Jay Jay's eyes got as big as grapes. "I don't know if I can," the little bird said. "I might fall!"

Cristy told the little bird, "Don't worry, I will catch you!" Cristy started by putting Jay Jay on the top tier of a bird bath and counted to three. "One Two Three."

Jay Jay bent down and pushed of with her tiny legs. Then, she opened her wings and leaped. "I'm doing it! I'm doing it!" she chirped. Jay Jay could see Cristy holding out her hand as a landing place. And with a clumsy thump Jay Jay grabbed ahold of Cristy's finger and held on tight.

Cristy was full of joy. "You did it Jay Jay! This was your first flight!"

Jay Jay was so proud of herself she fluffed her feathers. Everyday Cristy helped Jay Jay practice her flying.

One day while they were practicing flying, several of Cristy's dog friends came for a visit. "Hey there! What are you doing?" asked one of them.

JAY JAY

"I am learning to fly," Jay Jay responded proudly. "My mom says I am getting better flying every day. What is your name?" asked Jay Jay.

"My name is Charlee; this is my little brother Chuck, these are my big brothers Marty and Beau, and my big sister Mandy."

"It's very nice to meet you," said Jay Jay.

Charlee continued, "my family and our person are going for a walk. Would you like to come along, too?"

"My feet are so small," said Jay Jay. "How could I keep up with you?"

"Don't you know how to fly?" Charlee asked. "Just fly along beside us. By the way, Jay Jay, where is your mom?"

"She isn't around here right now, but I have a very sweet lady who has been teaching me all sorts of things. I would love for all of you to meet her!" responded Jay Jay.

Just then, they heard Clap, Clap, Clap, and a voice that was familiar to Jay Jay saying "Let's go for a walk!" a voice hollered.

"That's my mom," Charlee said. My family walks together every afternoon."

Charlee's mom turned the corner. Jay Jay's eyes lit up. "That's Cristy! I know her! She is the nice lady who has been taking care of me. Cristy is your mom?" asked Jay Jay.

"Yes, she is!" said Charlee. "So, YOU are the little one my mom has been spending so much time helping. She has been so sad, but now she is happy again, and very busy. Do you know that means? asked Charlee. You are part of our family!"

Jay Jay flew over to Cristy with excitement. Then, another person came around the corner. His name was Alvin. Jay Jay flew over and landed on his head. The little bird was So excited. She was part of a family. All of them began to go for their walk – Cristy, Alvin, Charlee, Chuck, Beau, Marty, Mandy, and flying right beside them was little Jay Jay.

Jay Jay flew from tree to tree, exploring all the new branches, and searching for bugs. They went for a walk together every day. Cristy was so happy!

Jay Jay and her new furry friends enjoyed spending time together. When special treat time came Jay Jay was there beside all the others waiting for her treat, too.

Jay Jay had a special tree where she liked to hide her treats.

She also had a special tree where she liked to sleep.

All the animals were best of friends. Jay Jay loved taking a long sip of water with Beau. When he walked away, she would jump into the bowl and splash, splash, splash the water.

The water was so much fun. Cristy always made sure Jay Jay had a big bowl of water for playing.

One day, while Jay Jay was splashing in the water, a big red Cardinal came said, "Who are you, and why are hanging around those people and those animals? Don't you know they will hurt you?"

But Jay Jay explained, "They are my family; they would never hurt me! They keep me safe"

The Cardinal said, Where is your feathered family? The birds should be the ones keeping you safe."

Jay Jay said, "I lost my feathered mommy when a big storm blew hard and my nest fell. My mommy Cristy and papa Alvin have taken care of me. She taught me how to eat, to fly, and to hunt. My furry friends and I go for a walk every day. We are a family."

The red bird shrugged her wings and flew off with the other red birds. They were all laughing. "She thinks she is a part of that family. Doesn't she know she is a bird?"

Jay Jay was sad and went to Cristy.

She asked her, "Am I a bird or a dog? I can wag my tail feathers like a dog; I can drink from a bowl like a dog; I can go for walks like a dog. Why can't my dog friends fly like me? Don't they know how? I can teach them!"

Cristy reached out and Jay Jay jumped up onto her hand. She bent over and kissed Jay Jay on the head. Cristy said, "Sweetheart they cannot fly because they do not have wings. You are special. You get to go way up high in the sky. They cannot do that. You are a bird and need to make some bird friends, too."

Cristy knew it was time for Jay Jay to learn the sounds of other Blue Jays. Cristy played Blue Jay calls for Jay Jay each day, and she listened. Each day Jay Jay learned what each of the sound meant. One day Cristy heard a sound that was not Jay Jay. The sound was different, and it got louder and louder. Then, she saw that the sound came from another Blue Jay. Cristy was really excited about the new bird. She called out to Jay Jay, "Hurry! Come here!"

The little bird flew over and tilted her head. She had heard the sound, too. "It sounds like me," chirped Jay Jay. She flew to a tree next to the Blue Jay. The two Jays looked at each other, and Jay Jay flew back over to Cristy. She said, "Can I go over and play with the other bird?"

"Of course," responded Cristy. She noticed Jay Jay had a twinkle in her eye.

As Jay Jay approached the other bird, Jay Jay said, "Hi, my name is Jay Jay; what's yours?"

"My name is Blue," he said. "You wanna play?"

"Sure," said Jay Jay. They flew off into the trees playing tag and swooped up bugs and berries.

Blue showed Jay Jay his diving skills, and Jay Jay showed her new friend her collection of acorns. They were best friends right away, and they played into the night.

The next morning when Cristy woke up and Jay Jay chirped and chirped with excitement. She told Cristy all about the adventures she had with her new friend. She ate her breakfast and hurried out to her tree yard to play again. She and Blue were best "best buds."

Cristy noticed that Jay Jay was spending more time with Blue. That made Cristy feel a little sad, but she was happy for Jay Jay.

One afternoon while Jay Jay and Blue were playing, a roar of thunder sounded. The sky began to get dark. The wind was getting stronger. Cristy called for Jay Jay, but there was no sign of her. She paced up and down; she worried about her little bird. The rain came down harder and harder. All she could think about was how much she loved the little bird, so she prayed for Jay Jay. As the rain went on, Cristy continued to worry. All through the night the rain kept coming down. She called out to Jay Jay, but still nothing happened. The next day, when the rain had stopped, she went outside and called again for Jay Jay. There was no response. Jay Jay was nowhere to be seen.

Several days passed with no sign of Jay Jay. Cristy was so worried she felt sick. She knew only one way to take the worry away. She kneeled and asked God to please give her a sign to ease her heart. She needed to know that Jay Jay was all right. She had not seen or heard Jay Jay for several days, which was not normal. They had been the best of buddies.

All at once Cristy heard a sound that got louder and louder. The sound was like Jay Jay's, but she heard another bird, too. Cristy ran as fast as she could down the path toward the chirping sound. She called out, "Jay Jay is that you?" A beam of sun lit up the clearing. On a limb covered with a primrose vine sat Jay Jay and her new friend Blue. "Jay Jay is that you?" Cristy cried out again.

"Yes Mom, I'm here," responded Jay Jay.

With a sigh of relief and a tear in her eye, Cristy smiled and said, "I have been so worried about you."

"Yes, I know," said Jay Jay.

"So why didn't you come home?' asked Cristy.

Then, Jay Jay explained everything. "I think I was only meant to be with you for a little while. God sent me to you through a tough storm in your life. While you were helping me, I was helping you. You loved me and kept me safe. You gave me confidence in myself and made me part of your family. You were so sad before and now you smile. God led me to come back and to tell you that I am grateful for all you have done. Now, it is time for me to start my own life and build my new family." Jay Jay continued, "God listened to your prayer. He knew how much losing your friend Zachery hurt you. He never wants to see his children cry, so he sent me to make you smile. God always listens and helps people in ways they don't expect. I love you Cristy and thank you! I will be around, so don't worry. Just keep smiling."

Jay Jay looked at Cristy and gave her a wink, as if to say, "You got this!" The little bird looked back at her and then back at Cristy. With a flutter of her wings, Jay Jay and Blue flew off together high above the trees.

At that moment Cristy knew all the pain she felt when she lost Zachery, disappeared the day Jay Jay came with the storm. Once again, she dropped to her knees. Instead of being angry with God, she was humbled by Him. She bowed her head and took a deep, cleansing breath. As she let her breath out, she felt all the sadness release. Cristy was overwhelmed. She had to smile as two words came from her, "Thank You!"

The End

What God Taught Me

Through the hurt of loosing Zachery I learned that God sends us gifts. The first one was having Zachery. A dog is the perfect example of how Gods unconditional love works. No matter what you look like, how you dress, how smart or challenged you are, a dog's love is the same. It never waivers. They just LOVE you.

The second thing I learned was when Jay Jay was so very small she had wings but didn't know what their purpose was for. God created her to fly. Her wings were to small and weak at first, but by surrounding herself with someone who loved her, and knew her potential, she was able to grow, gain strength and take that first big leap of faith. When Cristy holds her hand out to catch her, its the same way God is ALWAYS there for us if we fall. He never wants you to quit loving him. He never wants you to give up on yourself. Like a beautiful bird, you too have wings. They are meant to fly high to Heaven when your weak heart is made strong through his Son Jesus Christ. So I encourage you to grow, find your purpose, surround yourself with people who will hold you accountable, lift you up, serve others in need, and last but not least, FLY HIGH IN THE SKY Jesus is there with his arms spread wide waiting to catch you!

JAY JAY

JAY JAY

JAY JAY

JAY JAY

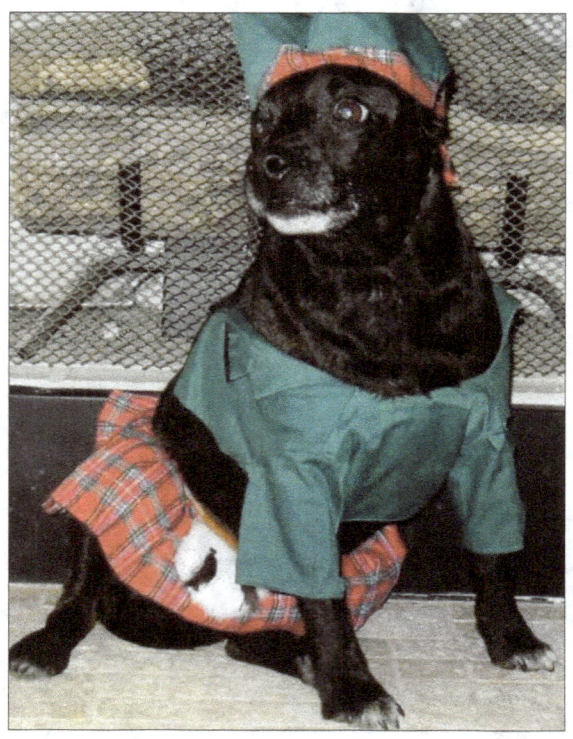

JAY JAY

JAY JAY

www.ingramcontent.com/pod-product-compliance
Lightning Source LLC
LaVergne TN
LVHW021950060526
838200LV00043B/1967